white wine

discovering, exploring, enjoying

RYLAND
PETERS
& SMALL
London New York

Jonathan Ray

photography by Alan Williams

white wine

discovering, exploring, enjoying

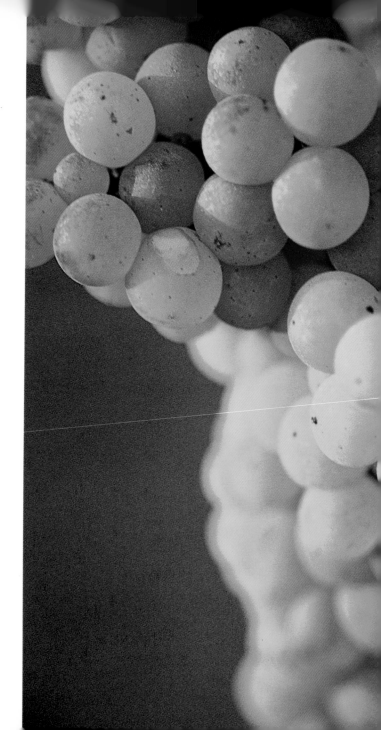

For Vickie, with love.

Designer Luis Peral-Aranda
Consultant Editor Anne Ryland
Editor Maddalena Bastianelli
Editorial Assistant Miriam Hyslop
Production Gavin Bradshaw
Art Director Gabriella Le Grazie
Publishing Director Alison Starling

Indexer Hilary Bird

First published in Great Britain in 2001
by Ryland Peters & Small, Inc.
519 Broadway, 5th Floor,
New York, NY 10012
www.rylandpeters.com

10 9 8 7 6 5 4 3 2 1

ISBN 1 84172 155 7

Printed in China

Contents

Introduction

White wines can be bone dry or richly sweet; they can be light and refreshing or headily alcoholic; and they can be still or sparkling. To complicate matters further, the world is producing more wine than ever before and in many more countries, so it is little wonder that some of us feel a trifle overwhelmed as we face the endless rows of bottles in the wine shop.

  It is important to resist the urge to panic: take a deep breath and simply start at the beginning. Climate, soil, and methods of production all make significant contributions to the way a wine tastes, but the most important factor by far is the grape itself, so a few hours spent differentiating between Sauvignon Blanc and Chardonnay, Riesling and Sémillon will be time well spent. Once you can identify the different grape varieties and the wines that they make, you will discover the wines you like and the wines you don't, and you will be well on your way to becoming an expert. Further research—which, let's be frank, will require some dedicated sluicing and slurping—will help you determine which wines make the ideal partners for which foods.

bottle shapes and sizes

In this age of designer chic, European wine producers are sticking less strictly to the traditional bottles of their respective regions, while producers from the New World are divided between those who use the shapes most associated with each particular variety and those who bottle their wines in whatever shape pleases them. Nevertheless, the shape and color of a wine bottle remain useful tools for identifying the style and type of wine inside.

As a rule, the sweet and dry white wines of Bordeaux, along with New World Sauvignon Blancs and Semillons, come in high shouldered bottles of green or clear glass; white burgundies, Chablis, white Rhônes, and many New World Chardonnays are in green bottles with sloping shoulders, while the aromatic wines of Alsace, Germany, and beyond come in tall, slender bottles. Those from Alsace are green, whereas German wines have a further distinction, in that wines from the Mosel (known as Moselles) come in green bottles and those from the Rhine (known as Hocks) come in brown bottles.

Apart from a couple of rare exceptions, champagne and other sparkling wines come in dark green bottles with sloping shoulders and a pronounced indentation in the base called a punt. Champagne producers are famous for using out-sized bottles for their wines, without which no grand celebration is complete. The sizes range from:

Quarter bottle = 187.5ml
Half bottle = 375ml
Bottle = 750ml
Magnum = 2 bottles
Double Magnum = 4 bottles
Jeroboam = 4 bottles
Rehoboam = 6 bottles
Methuselah = 8 bottles
Salmanazar = 12 bottles
Balthazar = 16 bottles
Nebuchadnezzar = 20 bottles

labels explained

Wine labels are there to help you, and if read correctly, they will tell you everything you need to know about the wine itself.

A label on the front of a bottle must, legally, tell you the following:

the wine's name

the size of the bottle

the vintage (if there is one)

the wine's alcoholic strength

the producer's name and address

the name of the bottler (if different from the producer)

the name of the shipper (if different from the importer)

the name of the importer

the wine's quality level

where the wine was bottled

country of origin

type of wine

what region and appellation the wine is from

some labels also include the grape variety

Wine imported into the United States, or made there and sold within, is also obliged to state whether or not sulfur dioxide was used in its production, and to display a government health warning concerning the hazards of drinking wine—not a word about the benefits...

Of all white wines, those from Germany have the most perplexing labels, and not only because they are often written in indecipherable Gothic script. Information which you will see on German wine labels includes the following terms for the six categories of ripeness:

Kabinett = the driest level of quality wine.

Spätlese = wines made from late-picked grapes.

Auslese = wines made from selected bunches of very ripe grapes.

Beerenauslese = wines made from individually selected grapes.

Trockenbeerenauslese = wines made from dried grapes or those attacked by "noble rot."

Eiswein = wines made from grapes picked when frozen which concentrates the sugar in the juice.

These terms can be linked to levels of sweetness, from Kabinett, the most dry, to the incredibly honeyed Trockenbeerenauslese and intensely sweet Eiswein.

Wine labels are there to help you, and if read correctly,
they will tell you everything you need to know about the wine itself.

single varietals and blends

A single varietal is a wine made wholly, or almost wholly, from a single type of grape, Chardonnay perhaps, Sauvignon Blanc, or Sylvaner. Rules differ from region to region; for example, in Australia 80 percent of the wine must come from the named variety, while in the United States it is 75 percent.

In Europe the trend has been to name the wines after the region of origin rather than after the variety— Alsace being a notable exception. It is here, therefore, that it pays to have a little knowledge: if, for example, you know that you like single varietal Chardonnays from California or Australia, say, then it is helpful to know that all white burgundies, such as Pouilly-Fuissé, Puligny-Montrachet, or Meursault, for example, are also single varietals, being 100 percent Chardonnay.

The art of blending is to marry the wines of two or more varieties together to make a wine greater than the sum of its parts. The process can also encompass different vintages, as with non-vintage champagnes or standard house white burgundies, blended in such a way as to make sure that they always taste the same. The blending of different varieties with each other occurs less frequently with white wines than it does with red wines. In France, for example, the great wines of the Loire, Sancerre and Pouilly Fumé, are 100 percent Sauvignon Blanc, while white burgundies and Chablis are 100 percent Chardonnay. Champagne is usually a blend of three varieties, but producers do also make champagnes from both Chardonnay and Pinot Noir on their own.

Some blends are only seen in the New World; in Australia Semillon/Chardonnay blends are common, but this is a combination which would be prohibited by the restrictive wine laws in most areas of France.

There are strong arguments both for blends and for single varietals, arguments that get trotted out whenever two or more wine makers are gathered together. Neither style is better than the other; they are just different; and just because you like the subtlety of this blend doesn't mean that you won't appreciate the purity of that single varietal.

The art of blending is to marry the wines of two or more varieties together to make a wine greater than the sum of its parts.

Chardonnay
Block L
Clone:
Wente 177 / AXR

c h a r d o n n a y

The world's most popular grape variety? Definitely. Purists might argue that Riesling makes the finer and the more elegant wine, but that is certainly not reflected in public opinion. Chardonnay is easy to grow, has good acid levels, high alcohol, ages well, blends happily with other varieties; and wine makers and wine drinkers can't get enough of it. It is rare to find a bad Chardonnay because it is difficult to make a poor wine from it.

Chardonnay is responsible for champagne and Chablis, and for such well-known white burgundies as Meursault, Puligny-Montrachet, Corton-Charlemagne, and Pouilly-Fuissé. Chardonnay can taste very different depending on where it is grown, because of variations in climate and wine makers' techniques. For example, Chardonnays from Burgundy tend to be more elegant and lean compared to the big, blousy wines from Australia or California,

Forget the red wine for once and drink a big oak-aged Chardonnay from Burgundy or Australia with a hearty meat casserole or roast veal, or a Chablis with cheeses such as Brie and Camembert.

where warmer climates result in riper grapes. But even in two neighboring areas there can be pronounced differences, for while white burgundies can be nutty or toasty, the wines of Chablis can be steely and flinty. Chardonnay does spectacularly well in Australia, New Zealand, South Africa, South America, Italy, and Spain. It is especially beloved by Californians, in whose State it is the most often planted grape variety. In fact, to many Americans, the word Chardonnay is synonymous with white wine, so ubiquitous is the variety. But despite these major successes elsewhere, Burgundy remains its spiritual home.

One cannot speak of Chardonnay without mentioning oak, with which it has a special relationship. Oak barrels draw out Chardonnay's best characteristics, and give the wine aromas of vanilla, toast, and nuts. Oaked and unoaked can be very different: try both.

There are many different types of Riesling with different names which can be confusing: in California the true Riesling is called Johannisberg Riesling, in Australia it is known as Rhine Riesling and in South Africa as Weisser Riesling.

riesling

True Riesling is the most elegant of grapes and is most at home in Germany, where all the top wines, be they sweet or dry, are Rieslings. The sweet wines are usually affected by noble rot and range in sweetness through Auslese and Beerenauslese to Trockenbeerenauslese. German Rieslings are often light in alcohol and age remarkably well, gaining rich honey flavors as they do so, and the grape should be instantly identifiable in the glass, marked out by its distinctive aromas of gasoline, peaches, melons, apples, and limes.

Remarkably, considering that it is regarded as one of the world's finest grapes—if not the finest—you won't find Riesling in France, other than in that quixotic and schizophrenic part of the country, Alsace. Here it is considered top dog and makes fresh, lively wines, which, while delicate, are fuller and higher in alcohol than those from neighboring Germany.

The grape is also widely grown in Austria, making dry, concentrated wines, and in Italy's Friuli and Alto Adige, where it makes light, elegant, and aromatic wines.

New Zealand grows Riesling in Marlborough, producing wines of excellent acidity and delicacy, and it features in Argentina and in Chile. Most of California is too warm to produce dry Riesling—the drinking public seems only to want Chardonnay anyway—but both Washington State and Ontario make use of the grape's preference for cool conditions to make wines of great delicacy. Some is grown in Australia in the Barossa, Eden, and Clare valleys.

Drier German Rieslings go well with Pacific Rim cooking and other spicy food, whilst the sweet ones are perfect with fruit, nuts, or desserts.

sauvignon blanc

Sauvignon Blanc is one of the world's major grape varieties, celebrated as much for its distinctive, steely dry single varietals as it is for the role it plays in the world's finest dessert wines.

France's most celebrated Sauvignon Blancs are Sancerre and Pouilly Fumé from the Loire, where producers don't believe in blending the variety, which they often call Blanc Fumé. Instead, they prefer to make single varietal wines, which are fermented and aged in stainless steel vats rather than oak, creating wines that are crisp and cleanly flavored with a smoky, mineral quality. Other lesser-known but good value Loire wines made from Sauvignon Blanc include Ménétou-Salon, Quincy, Reuilly, and Sauvignon de Touraine.

Sauvignon Blanc is more acidic than Chardonnay, and to some, this crispness is preferable to the soft butteriness of Chardonnay. The grape is notable for its aromas of freshly cut grass, black currant leaves, gooseberries, asparagus, and, remarkably but undeniably, cat's pee.

Impressive as it is on its own, arguably it is only when combined with Sémillon that Sauvignon Blanc achieves true greatness. In Bordeaux the dry wines of Entre-Deux-Mers and Graves are blends of Sauvignon Blanc and Sémillon (usually aged in oak), as are the great dessert wines of Sauternes and Barsac, and the lesser ones of Ste-Croix du Mont and Monbazillac.

Stunning Sauvignon Blancs come from New Zealand, where the wines of Sancerre and Pouilly Fumé are given an extremely close run for their money. In California, too, it flourishes, thanks to Robert Mondavi, who first pioneered the variety, terming it Fumé Blanc, and it is now second in popularity to Chardonnay, producing wines that tend to be less grassy than those of New Zealand or the Loire valley. The grape is also a great success in Chile and South Africa, where it is called Blanc Fumé.

Apart from the sweet wines and fuller dry wines of Bordeaux, most Sauvignon Blancs are best drunk young—within three or four years of the vintage is a good guide.

Being light, crisp, and refreshing, Sauvignon Blancs make excellent aperitifs as well as enhancing most poultry and fish dishes.

Single varietal Sémillon goes well with smoked fish such as trout, haddock, or mackerel.

sémillon

Sémillon produces deep yellow wines which are full-bodied, high in both alcohol and aroma, low in acid, and which age extremely well, being especially well-suited to oak. It is one of the great unsung grapes of the world, and many people consume it without ever having heard of it, most notably in the wines of Bordeaux, where Sémillon adds structure to the dry wines of Graves and the sweet ones of Sauternes and Barsac. It has recently become more prominent, thanks to its role in blended wines from the New World, most of which are labeled varietally.

Unblended, Sémillon is apt to make undistinguished, forgettable wines, but when it is combined with Sauvignon Blanc, great things happen. Sauvignon Blanc provides acidity and aromas, while Sémillon softens Sauvignon Blanc's rougher edges to make sublime wines that are often greater than either variety can make alone.

Sémillon is susceptible to noble rot and provides the lion's share of the blends that go to make up the finest Sauternes and Barsacs, whose rich, intensely honeyed and utterly delicious wines usually include about 80 percent Sémillon, 20 percent Sauvignon Blanc, and a slurp of Muscadelle.

Australia, where Semillon drops its accent and is sometimes called Hunter Valley Riesling, makes some fine single varietals, mainly in New South Wales and the Hunter Valley, perhaps proving to the doubters that the grape can stand alone. It is also blended very successfully with Chardonnay and makes fine dessert wines. Single varietal Sémillons are also made in South Africa, mainly in the Paarl, Wellington, and Franschhoek valleys, and in Chile, where it provides two-thirds of all white wine produced, much of it pretty basic—the grape tends to be fat and oily—little of which is exported.

Chenin Blanc is an extraordinary grape in that it can produce still and sparkling wine, sweet and dry wine, fortified wine and spirits.

chenin blanc

This grape comes originally from the Loire valley in France where it is often known as Pineau de la Loire, and where its versatility is much in evidence: it is here that it produces such wines as the dry Savennières from Anjou; the dry, the sparkling, or the utterly delicious sweet Vouvrays from Touraine; the late harvest Côteaux du Layons; and the sparkling wines of Saumur.

Gallons of indifferent and sharp table wine are made from Chenin Blanc in the Loire, too, proving perhaps that it is not at its best when made into a dry wine.

Its susceptibility to botrytis, the noble rot that concentrates the sugar in the grape, makes it ideal for producing dessert wines of great style and delicacy, the best of which can last for decades, gaining beautiful golden hues and rich honey flavors as they age. Chenin Blanc's high natural acidity is perfect for making sparkling wine, and it is an important component in the blend responsible for the world's oldest sparkling wine, Blanquette de Limoux from the Midi.

Chenin Blanc seems to thrive best in marginal climates, and it is grown successfully in New Zealand and in South Africa, where, known as Steen, it is the country's most popular variety, making light, dry, and refreshing wines. Elsewhere in the New World, Chenin Blanc is rarely accorded the respect it receives in the Loire or South Africa. In Australia it is used mainly for blending into commercial wines, while in California the clamor for Chardonnay and Sauvignon Blanc means that there is currently little consumer interest in it.

Nothing goes better with **strawberries** and cream

or a fruit flan than a sweet Vouvray.

Gewurztraminer goes well with strong cheese and spicy food such as Thai or Chinese cooking, as well as smoked salmon and Pacific Rim cooking.

Gewurztraminer may be the hardest variety to spell and to pronounce, but its deep golden color and exotic and heady aromas of litchi nuts, spice, flowers, peaches, and apricots are unforgettable, making it a cinch to spot at blind tastings.

Although it is grown throughout Europe and is supposed to have originated in Italy's Alto Adige (where it is still known as Traminer Aromatico), Gewurztraminer is most at home in Alsace. Here the variety is at its most pungent, making sweet-smelling but intensely dry wines, high in alcohol, low in acidity, and bursting with spicy flavors. In great years, rich and honeyed late harvest wines, known as *vendanges tardives*, are made as, too, in exceptional years, are botrytis-affected wines known as *séléction de grains nobles*.

Gewürz is the German word for spice, and Gewurztraminer is highly regarded both in Germany, especially in Rheinpfalz just over the border from Alsace, and in Austria. The grape does best in cool climates, and in the New World it is happiest in New Zealand, although there are some plantings in Australia, too. In California it is grown only in the cooler areas such as Carneros, Anderson Valley, Monterey County, and Mendocino, where it makes scented wines, noticeably softer and less spicy than those of Alsace. Some wines are also being made successfully in Oregon.

gewurztraminer

m a r s a n n e

Marsanne is a vigorous grape that produces deep-colored, brown-tinged wine high in alcohol with a distinctive and heady aroma reminiscent of apples, pears, glue, nuts, spice, and almonds. The grape's full flavor, coupled with a low acidity, means that it is ideal for blending, and the variety with which it is inextricably linked is Roussanne, which plays Tweedledum to Marsanne's Tweedledee. It is a highly successful partnership, responsible for such white wines of the northern Rhône as Côtes du Rhône Blanc, Crozes-Hermitage, Hermitage, and St-Joseph. Marsanne is also one of the grapes permitted in the blend that makes the southern Rhône's comparatively rare white Châteauneuf-du-Pape.

Although Marsanne is traditionally seen as making long-lived, full-bodied wines that can sometimes be dull when they are young, modern wine making techniques are changing such perceptions, and fruity, perfumed wines are produced for early consumption. When young, wines

A fine white Rhône is perfect with heavily sauced lobster or crab or with fish dishes such as grilled tuna or turbot.

are now flowery and aromatic, when old, they are rich and nutty; indeed, it seems nowadays that only in its middle-age is it dull. Increasingly grown in the Midi, Marsanne makes fleshy white wines in Cassis, and the dry, sweet, still and sparkling wines of St-Péray, just south of Cornas in the northern Rhône. It is a permitted ingredient in the northern Rhône's Syrah-dominated red Hermitage, and is grown successfully in Switzerland, where it is known as Ermitage Blanc.

As for the New World, Marsanne has been grown in Victoria in Australia since the 1860s, making big, long-lived wines, but it is seen only occasionally in California, where it appears as either single varietals or blended with its old Rhône chum, Roussanne.

pinot blanc

Found in almost every wine region in the world,
Pinot Blanc is best known in Alsace (where, unusually
for a French wine region, it is sold under its varietal name)
and in Italy where it is an important part of
the blend which makes Soave.

Pinot Blanc is not dissimilar to Chardonnay, to which it was once thought to be related,
although it is not nearly so complex, flavorsome, or sophisticated. At its best, it should be
fresh, lively, and appealing, with flavors of yeast and apples backed up by the faintest hints
of honey. But although it is invariably light and pleasing on the palate, it never really seems
to have a great deal to say. Its high acidity makes it ideal for making sparkling wines, and it
is used as the base for most of Alsace's fizzy Crémant d'Alsace.

Alsace Pinot Blanc goes especially well with fish pâté,
light salads, and pasta with seafood sauce.

In Alsace, Pinot Blanc also makes drinkable, if undramatic, dry white wines, the lightest of the region which, while well-regarded, are usually eclipsed by those of Pinot Gris. Modest amounts are also grown in Burgundy, usually for blending with Chardonnay into the region's basic white wine—Bourgogne Blanc. It is grown throughout Italy—where it is called Pinot Bianco—notably in the Veneto, Alto Adige, and Lombardy, where it makes pleasant sparkling wine. As Weissburgunder, Pinot Blanc is increasingly popular in Germany, making both dry and sweet wines—especially in Baden and Rheinpfalz—and it is grown throughout Austria, even being used to make botrytized Trockenbeerenauslese.

Pinot Blanc is ignored by much of the New World. Some is grown in Chile, and a few producers grow it successfully in California, although, confusingly, much of what is called Pinot Blanc in California is in fact Melon de Bourgogne.

Pinot Gris is low in acid and goes especially well with food; those from Alsace in particular are marvelous with that region's choucroute and cheese, as well as with charcuterie and hot or cold lobster.

pinot gris

Pinot Gris produces fragrant white wines of depth and substance, with styles ranging from crisp, light, and dry to rich, full, and honeyed. At its best, it makes a fine alternative to white burgundy and can be full-bodied enough to drink with dishes that are more usually accompanied by red wines. Although technically a white grape, Pinot Gris is a mutation of the red Pinot Noir, and it can produce wines that are almost rosé in color.

Pinot Gris thrives in Alsace (where it is sometimes still known as Tokay d'Alsace or Tokay Pinot-Gris), not only producing big, smoky, dry wines, but also the remarkably intense *vendanges tardives*. Around Touraine, in the Loire, it makes charming rosés, and in Switzerland's Valais it results in rich, full wines. While Pinot Gris is oily and fat in Alsace, it is lighter, spritzier, and more acidic in Italy, where—known

as Pinot Grigio—it is grown mainly in Friuli, Lombardy, and in small areas of Emilia-Romagna.

Germany grows more Pinot Gris (known there as Rulander) than any other country, producing juicy wines of low acidity and spicy aroma, most especially in Württemberg, Baden, and Rheinpfalz. Although it has yet to catch on in the New World, it is increasing in popularity in California, especially among those bored by the ubiquity of Chardonnay, and there are some plantings of Pinot Gris in Mexico and Willamette Valley in Oregon.

r o u s s a n n e

Roussanne is the more refined half of its celebrated vinous double act with Marsanne. In the northern Rhône in particular, the two grapes are inextricably linked, joining forces to produce the white versions of Hermitage, Crozes-Hermitage, and St-Joseph, as well as being used in small amounts in the red Hermitage blend, adding softness to the otherwise unblended Syrah. Roussanne is less widely grown than Marsanne, not least because it is prone to powdery mildew and rot and has an irregular yield, but it is the more stylish and polished of the two, and its wines age more gracefully. In the southern Rhône it is used in the blends that make both the red and the white Châteauneuf-du-Pape.

Roussanne is also grown in Languedoc-Roussillon, where the warm climate means that its tendency to ripen late is less of a problem than it is in the northern Rhône, or in Savoie in eastern France, where small amounts of single varietal Roussanne can be found if you can be bothered to look hard enough.

Roussanne has a spicier flavor than Marsanne, and while its wines are delicious when they are young, with a tendency to blossom in later years, they can, like those of Marsanne, be a bit grumpy in middle age. The two grapes also combine to make the Rhône's *méthode champenoise* wine, St-Péray, a full-flavored sparkler with an almost nutty taste.

White Rhônes go well with smoked eel, smoked salmon, and gravlax.

A fine Viognier is the perfect foil for grilled foie gras or pâté de foie gras, and its aromatic fruitiness and good acidity make it an excellent quaffer.

Viognier is suddenly a rather fashionable variety with both growers and drinkers alike, having gained its reputation by producing the extraordinarily intense dry white wines from the tiny vineyards of Château Grillet and Condrieu next door to Côte Rôtie in the northern Rhône. Restaurants that had never heard of Viognier five years ago, now stock several examples of the variety, which are well worth seeking out, although they are likely to be pricey.

Good Viogniers are big-boned beauties with alluring, but fleeting, scents of peaches and apricots, comparable in their headiness of aroma and pungency of flavor with Gewurztraminer. The less good examples, however, can be overpowering and lacking in finesse.

Viognier is something of a curiosity in that it has long been used as an aromatic addition to the great red wines of Côte Rôtie, being vinified alongside the red grape Syrah and comprising up to 20 percent of the final blend.

It is being seen more often in Italy and Australia as well as in other parts of France, such as Languedoc-Roussillon, where some notable single varietals are being produced and marketed under the name of the variety rather than the wines' geographic location. Viognier is also currently the flavor of the month in California, but despite its current popularity, the grape remains a rarity with very few plantings, and with some producers questioning whether or not investing in a potential passing fad is worth the hassle of the grape's low productivity and its susceptibility to disease.

viognier

aligoté

Aligoté is little seen outside Burgundy, where
it languishes in the shadow of Chardonnay,
and even there its popularity is waning. It is
grown mainly in the Mâconnais and Côte
Chalonnaise areas, where it makes zesty dry
white wine which is usually labeled
Bourgogne Aligoté. At its best, its wines can
be soft and creamy with hints of citrus, but all
too often it is acidic and short-lived.

In Burgundy, Aligoté is habitually used for
making Kir, a traditional drink in which the
wine's acidity is softened by a dash of Crème
de Cassis. It says a lot about a wine that even
the locals would rather not drink it unless it is
adulterated with black currant liqueur.
Nonetheless, the variety remains popular in
eastern Europe, especially Russia, where it is
often used to make sparkling wine.

Aligoté is best drunk as an aperitif, either on its own,
or, as mentioned above, as a Kir.

French country wines made from Colombard are ideal for knocking back, well chilled, at picnics or outdoors on late summer evenings.

Colombard originated in the Charente region of France, and it was used originally for distillation into Cognac and Armagnac. It has been largely supplanted in this role by Ugni Blanc, as Trebbiano is known there, so growers have turned to making it into simple, undemanding wines such as Vin de Pays des Côtes de Gascogne—crisp and spicy off-dry wines of high acidity and flowery perfume.

Remarkably, this productive but little-known variety is now one of the most widely planted varieties in California where—called French Colombard—it is prized for its ability to produce simple crisp wines in a warm climate. For similar reasons, it is also extensively grown in both Australia and South Africa, where it is often blended with Chenin Blanc to make everyday drinking wines or sparklers.

colombard

müller-thurgau

Müller-Thurgau is a hybrid variety created in 1882 by Dr Hermann Müller, from the Swiss canton of Thurgau, who, in crossing Riesling with Sylvaner, hoped to combine the quality of the former with the early-ripening capability of the latter. At its best, its wines are light, fresh, fruity, and fragrant; at worst they are bland, characterless, and utterly lacking in flavor.

Müller-Thurgau is the most planted variety in Germany making the infamous bottled bubblegum, Liebfraumilch. The grape ripens almost anywhere, producing enormous amounts of extremely dull, medium-dry, and some sweet, wine. The grape has a tendency to be a bit mousy in Germany though, and makes cleaner and fresher wines in Italy's Alto Adige, Luxembourg, and in England, where it is also the most planted variety.

The grape was the mainstay of New Zealand's embryonic wine industry, producers believing it to be the variety best suited to their climate, and indeed it probably makes better wine there than it does anywhere else. However, as the industry has grown and as tastes have become more sophisticated, so Chardonnay and Sauvignon Blanc have far outstripped Müller-Thurgau in terms of popularity.

Müller-Thurgau should be drunk on its own or with light, delicately flavored dishes.

m u s c a t

Muscat is thought to be the oldest variety known to man, its hundreds
of different incarnations producing many styles of wine.
It may sound odd, but Muscat is the only grape to produce wine that
actually tastes and smells of grapes.

One of the grape's best-known strains, Muscat Blanc à Petits Grains, is
responsible for the fortified Muscat de Beaumes-de-Venise from the
southern Rhône, and, blended with Clairette, the sparkling Clairette de Die
in the northern Rhône. In Italy it is the flavor behind Asti Spumante, and
in Greece it makes the dessert wines of Samos, Pátras, and Cephalonia.
In Australia, known as Brown Muscat or Frontignan, it makes delicious
fortified liqueur wines, as it does in California, where it is known as
Muscat Blanc, Muscat Canelli, or Muscat Frontignan.

Muscat Ottonel is grown in Alsace for heady dry wines and in Austria for
sublime dessert wines. Muscat of Alexandria is usually used for table
grapes, but in Spain it is used to make the heavy, sweet fortified wine,
Moscatel de Málaga and, in Portugal, Moscatel de Setúbal.

Orange Muscat and Muscat Hamburg are grown in Australia and California
for dessert wine, the latter, known as Black Muscat, only rarely being used.

All sweet muscats go well with desserts,
the Black Muscats and Orange Muscats being about the
only sweet wines that go well with chocolate.

s y l v a n e r

Sylvaner originated in Austria, in which country it still thrives, albeit less ubiquitously than before. Despite being edged out by its own ungrateful offspring—Müller-Thurgau—as the country's most planted variety, it is still much grown in Germany, mainly in Rheinhessen, Rheinpfalz, and Franken, in which latter region, where Riesling is difficult to ripen, it does especially well.

In France, Sylvaner is virtually unknown outside Alsace, where it makes easy-drinking, rather nondescript wines at the lower end of the price range. Even here it is planted with much less frequency than before. Switzerland remains true to the variety, especially in Valais where it is known as Johannisberg, making quaffable, refreshing wines of no great character. It used to be grown fairly widely in California, but in the charge to plant Sauvignon Blanc and Chardonnay, it has all but been forgotten.

Sylvaner from Alsace goes well with onion tarts and quiches and is delicious with bouillabaisse.

A fritto misto eaten on the waterfront of an Italian fishing village, washed down with an Orvieto or Frascati, is hard to beat.

trebbiano

No grape produces more of the world's wine than Trebbiano, and it remains the most widely planted variety in France, where it is known as Ugni Blanc. The grape is notorious for producing bland, nondescript wines of little character, so, on the principle that the worse the base wine, the better the brandy—much of it is used for distillation.

In Italy it appears blended with other varieties in such wines as Est! Est!! Est!!!, Frascati, Orvieto, Soave, Verdicchio, and Vernaccia di San Gimignano; it even finds its way into red Chianti.

Trebbiano is also grown in California—mainly in the San Joaquin valley—and in Mexico, in both cases chiefly being used for distillation.

champagne and
sparkling wines

Briefly, champagne is made by encouraging a second fermentation to occur in the bottle, by adding yeast and sugar to the previously blended Chardonnay, Pinot Meunier, and Pinot Noir. To be called champagne, the wine may only be made by this method, with these grapes, in the region of Champagne in northern France. The resulting sparkling wine is generally dry and white, although sweet champagnes, rosé

champagnes, and champagnes made solely from Chardonnay (known as Blanc de Blancs) or solely from a combination of Pinot Noir and Pinot Meunier (known as Blanc de Noirs) can also be found.

Most of the production is devoted to non-vintage (NV) champagne—wines from different vintages blended to

It is worth bearing in mind that the finest sparkling wines are often better—and are invariably cheaper—than the poorest champagnes.

guarantee consistency in each producer's distinctive house style. The rarer vintage champagne is the wine of one outstanding year only. Still wines are also made in Champagne but are little seen outside the region. "Extra Brut" is the driest category of sparkling champagne, followed by "Brut," both of which, are drier even than "Extra Dry" or "Extra Sec"; "Sec" is still less dry, "Demi-Sec" is noticeably sweet, while "Doux" is the sweetest of all.

Sparkling wines are made all over the world using the champagne method, with Germany, New Zealand, California, the Loire, Spain, Italy, and Australia all producing extremely good ones, usually from Chardonnay and Pinot Noir, although other grapes such as Riesling, Chenin Blanc, and Aligoté are also used. Such producers will label their wines *méthode champenoise* or *méthode traditionelle* to distinguish their products from poorer wines made by cheaper methods.

dessert wines

The world's most celebrated dessert wines come from Sauternes and Barsac in Bordeaux, and from Germany and Hungary, although fine examples are also produced in Alsace, Austria, Australia, California, Canada, and Greece.

A dessert wine can be sweet for a number of reasons: it might be a "late-picked" wine, known in France as *vendange tardive*, made from extremely ripe grapes picked late in the season when their sweetness is most concentrated, or it might be a *vin doux naturel* such as Muscat de Beaumes-de-Venise, whose fermentation has been stopped by the addition of brandy before all the sugar has turned to alcohol.

Alternatively, like a Sauternes or Barsac, it might have been made from grapes affected by noble rot, the name given to *botrytis cinerea*—known as *pourriture noble* in France and *edelfäule* in Germany. Botrytis is a mold which, in areas prone to damp, humid conditions, attacks certain grapes, making them shrivel and rot, thus concentrating their flavor and their sugars. Sauvignon Blanc, Sémillon, Chenin Blanc, and Gewurztraminer in France and Riesling in Germany are particularly susceptible, and, the grapes having been picked individually by hand, produce dessert wines high in alcohol and richness of flavor. It is a laborious and wasteful process, however, for while a single vine is capable of producing a bottle of ordinary wine, it will only produce one glass of Sauternes.

Desserts are often greatly improved by an accompanying glass of dessert wine—a German Trockenbeerenauslese, perhaps, or a sweet Vouvray. But beware, some fruit can make such wines taste less sweet than usual, and chocolate in particular is a tricky partner for wine, having a tendency to overwhelm even the greatest of dessert wines. But don't feel you have to keep the Sauternes, Barsac, or Muscat de Beaumes-de-Venise for the end of a meal: do as the French do, and drink them well-chilled with rich appetizers such as pâté de foie gras.

sherry

There are **several varieties** of sherry to suit all manner of tastes, which can be drunk on many **different occasions**.

Sherry, comes from the deep southwestern corner of Spain and takes its name from the town of Jerez de la Frontera. It is a fortified white wine made from Moscatel, Palomino, and Pedro Ximénez which is fermented in barrels above ground and upon the surface of which a filmy growth called "flor" grows, from which the wine gets its unique flavor.

Once fermented and then fortified, the barrels of wine are categorized depending on the aging potential of each wine. The new wine is then added to a line of anything up to 100 butts, known as the solera—a system that involves the topping up of older barrels with younger wine of the same style so the wine is continuously being blended, guaranteeing that it always tastes the same—while fully mature wine ready for blending comes out of the other end.

Although the wines are usually sold under brand names such as Tio Pepe (from Gonzalez Byass) or La Ina (from Domecq), the label will also state what style of sherry it is. The appetizingly tangy Manzanilla, which comes from Jerez's neighboring town of Sanlúcar de Barrameda, and Fino are the driest sherries, whose zip and freshness make them great kick-starters for the appetite. Amontillado is effectively an aged Fino, whose time spent in cask imparts a medium-dry nuttiness to the flavor. Cream sherry is the sweetest, but it tends to lack the richness and fullness of flavor to be found in a top-class Oloroso, which, although packed with concentrated fruit aromas, can be dry or sweet to the taste.

v i n t a g e s

Differences between wines are caused by the soil, the grapes, the way in which they were made, and above all by the weather. In places such as California or Australia, blessed with constant temperatures and clement weather, variations between different years are less pronounced than they are in Europe, where a late frost, hailstorm, or lack of sunshine can mean the difference between success and failure for a harvest.

If a blend of two or more vintages is used, the resultant wine will be known as non-vintage or NV, and will show no date on the label.

The listing of a vintage date on a bottle of wine must not be taken as a guarantee of quality—except with fine wines—but rather as simply a matter of record and a note of the wine's age.

Recent fine vintages for white burgundy include 1985, 1986, 1988, 1989, 1990, 1992, 1993, 1995, 1996.

Recent fine vintages for Sauternes include 1986, 1988, 1989, 1990, 1996, 1997.

Vintage champagne (like vintage port) is only made in exceptional years, the most recent being 1985, 1988, 1990, 1993, 1995, 1996.

a g i n g

Aging is the process by which wines settle down after fermentation, mature, and improve; and nowhere do they do this better than in oak barrels. Great differences are achieved by the size of the barrel, the type of oak used (usually limousin or tronçais), and by whether it is old oak or new, or a combination of the two. New oak contains vanillin, which leads wines that have been in oak for any length of time to smell of vanilla.

Chardonnay is particularly well suited to spending time in oak,

by which process it takes on a deeper color and fuller, softer, vanillalike flavors. Indeed, it is extraordinary how much flavor Chardonnay does get from oak.

Some producers prefer not to use oak, because they feel that it imparts too much flavor to their wines, so they use stainless steel instead. Other producers feel that oak is essential, while some even use oak chips as a rather unsatisfactory short-cut method to imparting the unique flavor associated with oak.

laying down

While many red wines gain from being kept for several years, allowing the tannins to soften and the fruit to develop with the passage of time, there are only a few white wines that benefit from being laid down. This is partly because most white wine that is bought from the liquor store is ready to drink and will not improve or increase in value, and partly because the majority of white wines do not need long to mature. White burgundies, Chablis, white Rhônes, German and Alsace wines, the dessert wines of Sauternes and Barsac, and vintage champagnes are all worth laying down for a few years, provided that they are of mid- to top-quality and they are from fine years. As they age, such wines will develop deeper colors and complex toasty, nutty flavors, along with rich honey tones in the case of the dessert wines. With luck, they might also increase in value.

wine in restaurants

A good restaurant should pride itself on having top-quality wine list, and you should feel confident about ordering the wines on it.

When the bottle arrives, check that it is exactly what you ordered (vintage, château, etc.), make sure that it is opened at the table, and check that its temperature is satisfactory. If the white is too warm, ask for it to be put in an ice bucket.

Unless you have ordered house wine, it is likely that you will be asked to taste the wine. There is no need to feel awkward. Relax: almost everything that could possibly be wrong with the wine can be discovered by looking at it in the glass and by smelling it. It should look bright and clear, and in the rare event of something being wrong with it, it will smell moldy, stale, or tainted. It is hard to think of any wine—other than, perhaps, white Rhône, which can often smell like sherry—that doesn't flutter its eyelids at you. Many restaurants now sell wine by the glass—especially useful if you fancy a slurp of dessert wine with the final course.

A good restaurant should pride itself on having a top-quality wine list, and you should feel confident about ordering the wines on it.

food and wine

There is only one rule to bear in mind when matching wine with food, and that is, don't be afraid to experiment. Trial and error is the only way to find that perfect pairing where wine and food combine in harmony, each enhancing the other. Generally speaking, the lighter the dish, the lighter the wine should be and the heavier the dish, the heavier the wine, but everyone's taste differs, and while you should always bear in mind the experience of those who have trodden this path before you, the only way to find out what you like is to try it for yourself. The pairings listed below should be considered as no more than suggestions and ideas to set you on your way; wine was created to accompany food, and you will be surprised at some of the unlikely pairings that succeed. Be brave and enjoy!

Aperitifs Champagne or sparkling wine if the occasion demands it, alternatively, a well-chilled Fino or Manzanilla will kick-start the most jaded of appetites.

Beef
BEEF STEWS A big, oak-aged Chardonnay from Burgundy or California.
ROAST BEEF Red might be the obvious choice, but a Pinot Gris from Alsace has the weight and the depth of flavor to make a very decent substitute.
Canapés Sparkling wine, chilled Fino or Manzanilla sherry or any light, dry white wine.
Charcuterie Ham and salami go especially well with full-flavored wines such as Alsace Pinot Gris, Australian Semillon/Chardonnay, California Chardonnay or New Zealand Sauvignon Blanc.
PROSCIUTTO WITH MELON Try an Italian white such as Orvieto, Frascati, or Verdicchio.

Cheese
BLUE CHEESE (such as Stilton, Dolcelatte, Gorgonzola) An intensely sweet Sauternes or Beerenauslese.
GOAT CHEESE Try a bone-dry white wine or an intensely sweet one instead of the more usual red.
SOFT CHEESE (such as Brie, Camembert) Surprisingly, an unoaked Chardonnay from Chablis, say, or New Zealand, often makes a better partner to such cheese than a red wine would.

STRONG CHEESE (such as Münster or Roquefort) A late harvest Gewurztraminer from Alsace, or an Icewine from Canada—both served well-chilled—will make you wonder why you never tried such a pairing before.

Chicken
CHICKEN IN CREAMY SAUCES Such dishes need something with a bit of character, such as an Alsace Pinot Gris or a New Zealand Sauvignon Blanc.
CHICKEN LIVER PÂTÉ A dry white from Burgundy or Bordeaux, or even a Viognier.
COLD CHICKEN Any white wine with a bit of oomph will do, such as a white Rhône or a white Rioja.
FRIED CHICKEN Almost any wine you can think of would work here, so be daring and experiment.
ROAST CHICKEN A full-flavored white wine such as a New World Chardonnay or mature white burgundy will hit the spot.

Chinese food A medium-dry German Riesling or a California Chardonnay can't be bettered.

Cookies An Amontillado sherry or a medium-dry Vouvray.

Dessserts
CAKE Oloroso or cream sherry.

CHOCOLATE PUDDINGS The only wines that can really stand up to chocolate are the Black Muscats and Orange Muscats of California and Australia.

FRESH FRUIT Fruit can be tricky, so stick to a sweet Coteaux du Layon or Vouvray.

FRUIT TARTS German or Austrian Beerenauslese, or a late harvest Alsace Gewurztraminer.

STRAWBERRIES AND CREAM A sweet Vouvray or a sweet sparkler like Asti Spumante.

ICE CREAM AND SHERBERT Take a break from the wine here.

Duck

ROAST DUCK An aromatic Viognier, top-quality Chablis, or Alsace.

SEARED DUCK BREAST Something full-bodied and flavorsome like a German Spätlese or Alsace Pinot Gris.

Egg dishes Eggs aren't the ideal partners for wine, but a plate of scrambled eggs and smoked salmon always seems to demand champagne or top-quality sparkling wine.

QUICHE Anything from Alsace.

Fish

BASS Chablis, or a New Zealand Chardonnay.

BOUILLABAISSE Any dry wine from the Loire—a Pouilly Fumé or Sancerre if you are in funds, a Muscadet or Sauvignon de Touraine if you are not.

BROILED SHRIMP Any dry white wine will do.

COD A good quality dry white burgundy or New World Chardonnay.

GRILLED SOLE OR FLOUNDER Such a simple dish will allow any top-quality wine to show off, such as the best white burgundy or Chablis you can lay your hands on.

GRILLED TROUT Try an English wine.

GRILLED TURBOT AND TUNA A white Rhône or Rioja works well.

FISH IN CREAM SAUCE Such dishes are well-partnered by Riesling from Alsace or Germany.

FISH PÂTÉ An aromatic Viognier or an Alsace Riesling would be perfect.

FISH PIE Try a Sauvignon Blanc from New Zealand or Chile.

FRIED FISH A light, dry Italian such as Orvieto or Frascati.

SMOKED EEL, MACKEREL, AND SALMON Australian Semillon or Alsace Gewurztraminer.

SMOKED HADDOCK OR COD White Rhône or full-bodied Chardonnay.

Foie gras Top-quality sweet wine such as Sauternes or a dry Viognier.

Goose Something big and highly-flavored is needed, such as an Alsace Pinot Gris or an Hermitage Blanc. You might even consider an off-dry Riesling such as a German Spätlese.

Greek food Retsina is the obvious choice for taramasalata and calamari,

but since it is something of an acquired taste, you might prefer a Muscadet or an Italian Chardonnay.

Ham (*See* Charcuterie)

Indian food An ice-cold medium-dry Vouvray or an off-dry Orvieto, unless you are sticking to beer.

Lamb

GRILLED LAMB CHOPS A big, butch New World Chardonnay or white Rhône.

ROAST LAMB Something full-flavored but dry is needed if you are eschewing red wine, an Hermitage Blanc perhaps.

Mexican food Sauvignon Blancs from Chile, California, or New Zealand probably work best.

North African food Best stick to full-bodied wines from the Rhône or the New World.

Nuts A Fino or Manzanilla sherry.

Olives Dry sherry works best of all.

Pacific Rim Riesling works well with this style of cooking, as does almost anything from Alsace.

Pasta

WITH CREAMY SAUCE A crisp, dry Italian white is ideal.

WITH SEAFOOD SAUCE Almost any white wine from Italy, such as Orvieto, Frascati, Soave, or Verdicchio.

WITH PESTO SAUCE Ditto, although a simple unoaked Chardonnay works well, too.

Picnics A well-chilled French country wine such as a Côtes de Gascogne if there are lots of people, but treat yourselves to vintage champagne if there are only two of you.

Pizza To be authentic, an Orvieto, Frascati or Pinot Grigio should be chosen, but in reality almost any white wine goes well.

Pork

PORK CHOPS Red wine would be the obvious choice, but no full-bodied white will let you down—why not try Viognier?

ROAST PORK Any full-bodied white wine will do.

Risotto Italian Pinot Grigio.

Salads Something dry and light, like a Muscadet or Chilean Sauvignon Blanc.

Seafood

CAVIAR If you are eating caviar, it probably means that someone else is paying, so insist on champagne.

CLAMS Almost any dry white wine goes well with clams, be they raw or steamed—a Muscadet perhaps, or a Chilean Sauvignon Blanc.

DUNGENESS CRABS California Fumé Blanc, or Chardonnay.

LOBSTER THERMIDOR This dish gives you the chance to open an old white burgundy, top-quality New World Chardonnay, or Hermitage Blanc.

MUSSELS Muscadet or Belgian beer.

SAUTÉED SCALLOPS Dry German Riesling or New Zealand Sauvignon Blanc.

STEAMED MAINE LOBSTER The lobster deserves nothing less than a top-quality white burgundy or California Chardonnay. Even champagne wouldn't be out of place.

RAW OYSTERS ON THE HALFSHELL Sancerre, Pouilly Fumé, or Black Velvet (champagne and draft Guinness, half and half, in a tankard).

Soup It does depend on what sort of soup it is, but dry sherry usually works well.

Sushi and sashimi Sake (served hot) or a full-flavored New World Chardonnay would fit the bill.

Tapas Sherry, of course (although any decent white wine will do).

Thai food Spicy food like this needs a spicy Gewurztraminer.

Turkey Any decent white wine with body and character goes well with turkey, roasted or cold.

Veal

ROAST VEAL A big, oak-aged Chardonnay from Burgundy or Australia.

GRILLED VEAL CHOPS White Rhône, Alsace Pinot Gris, or a full-flavored Italian Chardonnay.

VEAL IN CREAM SAUCE Pouilly Fumé or Sancerre or even Alsace Riesling.

VEAL SCALLOPINE A well-made Riesling would fit the bill here.

Vegetables

ROAST VEGETABLES An oaky Chardonnay from Australia or California is ideal.

quality classifications

Wine laws are very strict, and their purpose is twofold: to protect the producer by making sure his region's reputation isn't undermined by the unscrupulous practices of some rogue, and to protect the consumer by guaranteeing the basic quality and character of the wine.

In general, France's stringent *Appellation d'Origine Contrôlée* (AOC) laws give a guarantee as to a wine's origins and authenticity as to grape variety, but without guaranteeing quality. The categories below AOC are *Vins Délimité de Qualité Supérieure* (VDQS), *Vin de Pays,* and *Vin de Table*: these are for lower-quality wines and have less rigid production restrictions.

Italy has a similar system, the *Denominazione di Origine Controllata* (DOC), although many top producers consider it too restrictive and make great wines that are obliged to be classified as *Vino da Tavola*. A new classification, *Indicazione Geografica Tipica* (IGT) has been introduced to alleviate some of the confusion.

Germany's classifications of quality refer to the ripeness of the grapes and therefore to the sweetness of the wine.

In Burgundy, a classification of *Premiers Crus* and *Grands Crus* identify the best vineyards, based on location, while Alsace contains elements of both systems.

Virtually every European wine-growing region has its own rules as to which grapes may be used where and by what method they might be grown and vinified. Where such rules do not exist, individual producers often create a structure of their own.

Spain and Italy designate their wines *Reserva* or *Riserva* to indicate a certain period in oak, a treatment usually confined to only the best wines, unlike the French, whose categories relate to location.

New World wines are not subject to such strict restrictions, something that is often more than made up for by producers giving extraordinarily detailed information on the back label.

storing   serving

Only a few white wines improve with age: top-class white burgundy, for example, or Chablis, Sauternes, and vintage champagne. Most white wine is likely to be for immediate consumption.

Store white wines as you would red wines, on their sides somewhere cool and dark and away from damp, vibration, and strong smells. Wooden wine racks are readily available and can be shaped to fit the most awkward spots. Alternatively, you can do a lot worse than use a cardboard wine box lying on its side.

White wine is best served chilled rather than ice cold; an hour in the refrigerator should be fine.

To open a bottle of champagne, remove the foil and wire, and hold the bottle at a slant with the base of the bottle in your strong hand, the cork in the other. Hold the cork firmly while twisting the bottle slowly, taking care that you don't shake it. Ease the cork out gently, covering it with the palm of your hand, while making sure a glass is nearby in case the wine should froth out. Serve in tall glasses to preserve the bubbles that the wine maker has striven so hard to achieve.

t a s t i n g

Fill no more than a quarter of your glass and look at the wine, preferably against a white background. The wine should be clear and bright without any cloudiness or haziness. Holding the stem, swirl the glass around to release the bouquet. Take a good sniff; it should smell clean and fresh. Almost anything that might be wrong with a wine can be detected on the nose, by odors of mustiness perhaps, or dampness.

Take a mouthful of the wine, drawing air into the mouth as you do so. Roll the liquid around your tongue and then spit or swallow. What is it like? Is it sweet or dry, light or full-bodied? Does it remind you of anything? The taste of a fine wine remains in the mouth, and its many components—its acidity, alcohol, fruit, and tannin—should have combined so pleasantly that you want nothing more than to take another sip.

glossary

Acid/acidity Acids occur naturally in wine and are crucial in giving it character and structure, and in helping it to age.

Aroma The varietal smell of a wine.

Balance A wine's harmonious combination of acids, tannins, alcohol, fruit, and flavor.

Bereich (German) Term for a wine-producing district.

Bianco (Italian) White.

Blanc (French) White.

Blanc de blancs (French) A white wine made only from white grapes.

Blanc de noirs (French) A white wine made only from black (red) grapes.

Blanco (Spanish) White.

Blind tasting A tasting of wines at which the labels and shapes of the bottles are concealed from the tasters.

Bodega (Spanish) Winery.

Body The weight and structure of a wine.

Botrytis cinerea A fungus which, when it shrivels and rots white grapes, concentrates their flavors and sugars, leading to dessert wines high in alcohol and richness of flavor. Also known as noble rot, *pourriture noble,* and *edelfäule.*

Bouquet The complex scent of a wine that develops as it matures.

Cantina (Italian) Winery or cellar.

Cave (French) Cellar.

Cellar book A useful way of noting what wines you have bought, from where, and at what price, as well as recording when you consumed them and what they tasted like.

Cepa (Spanish) Term for vine variety.

Cépage (French) Term for vine variety.

Chai (French) Place for storing wine.

Château (French) Term for a wine-growing property— chiefly used in Bordeaux.

Clos (French) Enclosed vineyard.

Corkage Charge per bottle levied on those customers in restaurants who bring in their own wine to drink.

Corked Condition, indicated by a musty odor, where a wine has been contaminated by a faulty cork.

Cosecha (Spanish) Vintage.

Côte (French) Hillside of vineyards.

Crémant (French) Semi-sparkling.

Cru (French) Growth or vineyard.

Cuvée (French) A blended wine or a special selection.

Demi-sec (French) Semisweet.

Dolce (Italian) Sweet.

Domaine (French) Property or estate.

Doux (French) Sweet.

Dulce (Spanish) Sweet.

Fermentation The transformation of grape juice into wine, whereby yeasts— naturally present in grapes and occasionally added in cultured form—convert sugars into alcohol.

Frizzante (Italian) Semi-sparkling.

Grand cru (French) Term used for top-quality wines in Alsace, Bordeaux, Burgundy, and Champagne.

Halbtrocken (German) Medium dry.

Horizontal tasting A tasting of several different wines that all come from the same vintage.

Jahrgang (German) Vintage.

Keller (German) Cellar.

Landwein (German) A level of quality wine just above simple table wine, equivalent to the French *vin de pays.*

Late harvest Very ripe grapes picked late, when their sweetness is most concentrated.

Méthode champenoise The method—involving a secondary fermentation in the bottle—by which champagne and top-quality sparkling wines are made.

Moelleux (French) Sweet.

Mousse (French) The effervescence that froths in a glass of sparkling wine as it is poured, and which seems to wink at you.

Mousseux (French) Sparkling.

Négociant (French) Wine merchant, shipper, or grower who buys wine or grapes in bulk from several sources before vinifying and/or bottling the wine himself.

Non-vintage (NV) Term applied to a wine that is a blend of more than one vintage, notably champagne.

Nose The overall sense given off by a wine on being smelled. It is not just the wine's scent; the nose also conveys information about the wine's wellbeing.

Oak Much wine is aged in oak barrels, something that is typified by whiffs of vanilla or cedar.

Oxidized Term used to describe wine that has deteriorated owing to overlong exposure to air.

Perlant (French) A term that refers to a wine with the faintest of sparkles in it.

Perlwein (German) A type of low-grade semisparkling wine.

Pétillant (French) Slightly sparkling.

Phylloxera An aphidlike insect that attacks the roots of vines with disastrous results.

Récolte (French) Crop or vintage.

Sec (French) Dry.

Secco (Italian) Dry.

Seco (Spanish/Portuguese) Dry.

Sekt (German) The German, not for dry—which is trocken —but for sparkling wine.

Sommelier Wine waiter.

Spittoon Receptacle into which one expectorates wine at a wine tasting.

Spritzer A refreshing drink made from white wine and soda or sparkling club water and usually served with ice.

Spumante (Italian) Sparkling.

Sur lie Term frequently given in the Loire, to the process of aging wines on their lees or sediment prior

to bottling, resulting in a greater depth of flavor.

Tafelwien (German) Table wine.

Trocken (German) Dry.

Varietal A wine named after the grape (or the major constituent grape) from which it is made.

Variety Term for each distinctive breed of grape.

Vendange (French) Harvest or vintage.

Vendange tardive (French) Late harvest.

Vendemmia (Italian) Harvest or vintage.

Vendimia (Spanish) Harvest or vintage.

Vertical tasting A tasting of several wines from the same property which all come from different vintages.

Vigneron (French) Wine grower.

Vin de pays (French) Country wine of a level higher than table wine.

Vin de table (French) Table wine.

Vin doux naturel (VDN) (French) A fortified wine that has been sweetened and strengthened by the addition of alcohol, either before or after fermentation.

Vin ordinaire (French) Basic wine not subject to any regulations.

Vinification Wine making.

Vino da tavola (Italian) Table wine.

Vino de mesa (Spanish) Table wine.

Vintage Both the year of the grape harvest itself as well as the wine made from those grapes.

Viticulture Cultivation of grapes.

index

acknowledgments

I would like to thank Anne Ryland for coming up with the idea in the first place, and Alison Starling, Gabriella Le Grazie, Luis Peral-Aranda, and Maddalena Bastianelli for making the project such an enjoyable one. I am also most grateful to Judith Murray, to David Roberts MW, and to Alan Williams for his beautiful photographs, several of which were taken at the restaurant Villandry and the wine merchant Berry Bros and Rudd Ltd, to whom also many thanks. Finally, of course, I would like to thank my wife Marina, ever patient and ever wise, and without whom...

Villandry
170 Great Portland Street
London W1N 5TB
020 7631 3131

Berry Bros & Rudd Ltd
3 St. James's Street
London SW1A 1EG
020 7396 9600

The author and publisher would also like to thank the following companies for allowing us to photograph their vineyards, wineries and cellars.

AUSTRALIA
Barossa Valley, South Australia
d'Arenberg, McLaren Vale, South Australia
Rockford Vineyards, Barossa Valley, South Australia

CALIFORNIA
Beringer Wine Estates, St Helena, Napa Valley
De Loach Vineyards, Sonoma Valley
Heitz Wine Cellars, St Helena, Napa Valley
Schramsberg Vineyards, Napa Valley